D1541975

The Contra Mundum Collection is a series of writings that counter the jetsam and flotsam of rank secularism and liberty-strangling socialism.
Enjoy.

High Praise for Doug Giles

"Doug Giles is a good man, and his bambinas are fearless. His girls Hannah and Regis Giles are indefatigable. I admire the Giles clan from afar."
— *Dennis Miller* —

"Doug Giles must be some kind of a great guy if CNN wants to impugn him."
— *Rush Limbaugh* —

"Doug Giles is a substantive and funny force for traditional values."
— *Ann Coulter* —

"Doug Giles speaks the truth ... he's a societal watchdog ... a funny bastard."
— *Ted Nugent* —

"Doug is funny and insightful. Giles is always spot-on with his analysis and so incredibly hilarious, as well. Whether you're 15 or 50, if you love God and America, Doug Giles is for you!"
— *Jason Mattera, NYT best-selling author of **Obama Zombies** and Editor-in-Chief, **Human Events** —*

"Doug is a raucous and rowdy mix of old-school, traditional conservative values with the kind of eff-you attitude folks like Ted Nugent have made millions on. He's one part rebellious rock star, one part crusading missionary, and another part rough rider."
— *S. E. Cupp, NYT best-selling author of **Why You're Wrong About The Right** and Co-Host of MSNBC's, **The Cycle** —*

Doug Giles

Raising Boys Feminists Will Hate

Volume 1 of the Doug Giles
Contra Mundum Collection

Copyright 2012, Doug Giles, All Rights Reserved

No part of this book may be reproduced, stored in a retrieval system, or transmitted by any means without the written permission of the author.

Published by White Feather Press. (www.whitefeatherpress.com)

ISBN 978-16180804-5-5

Printed in the United States of America

Cover design by David Bugnon and mopolis.com

Front cover sketch by Doug Giles

White Feather Press

Reaffirming Faith in God, Family, and Country!

Dedication

This screed is dedicated to fathers who enjoy living in the God-blessed testosterone fog and who wish to raise their sons to be men and not Nancy-boys.

Special thanks to Douglas Wilson whose book, *Future Men*, proved to me via the scripture that I am right in my assessment of what boys need to become men.

CONTENTS

Part I - Raising Boys that Feminists Will Hate 1

Part II - Raising Boys With Masculine Values 7

Part III - Raising Boys Impervious to Feminist Pressure...................13

Part IV - Raising Boys with the Masculinity of Christ 21

Part V - Parents Obsessed with Texting + Ignored Kids = Hell to Pay 27

Introduction

Feminists would love nothing more than to take your son and eradicate his masculine uniqueness. They hate men, and therefore, they will hate your son. That is, of course, assuming that you, the parent, intend to raise your son to be a man instead of a rouged and lipsticked, male *American Idol* hopeful. Get it right, parental unit: in the coming days you will be facing female chauvinist pigs who have sick designs for your dear son in culture, in the classroom and in a lot of churches.

These whacked women actually believe that masculinity, the male composition, and a guy's hormones cause boys to become wicked oppressors, sexually abusive and brutal beasts; and they have the inflated stats, the re-written history books and the hysterical spin to prove it.

Your daunting mission is to go against the grain, stand up to the radical feminists, and raise your little man into a lion, capable of leading the next generation into a moral culture of God, family and country.

Doug Giles

Doug Giles Tip # 1

Keep your boy far away
from pop culture.

PART I
RAISING BOYS THAT
FEMINISTS WILL HATE

PARENT, IF YOU HAVE A YOUNG SON and you want him to grow up to be a man, then you need to keep him away from pop culture, public school and a lot of Nancy Boy churches.   If metrosexual pop culture, feminized public schools and the effeminate branches of evanjellycalism lay their sissy hands on him, you can kiss his masculinity good-bye because they will morph him into a dandy.

Yeah, mom and dad, if – if – you dare to raise your boy as a classic boy in this castrated epoch, then you've got a task that's more difficult than getting a drunk to hit the urinal at Chili's.

Get it right mom and dad, you are rowing against the flotsam and jetsam of Sally River. I hope you have a sturdy ideological paddle and some serious forearms, because our crap culture is determined to keep your boy and his testosterone at bay. Yes, they will attempt at every turn to either drill it or drug it out of him.

Parent, if you're groping for a creedal oar to help you stem the increasingly stem-less effete environment, I've got a novel idea: Howzabout going back to the Bible, in particular the book of Genesis, and see what God the Father created His initial kid to be. Check this out.

Gen.1.24-28:

Then God said, "Let the earth bring forth the living creature according to its kind: cattle and creeping thing and beast of the earth, each according to its kind"; and it was so. And God made the beast of the earth according to its kind, cattle according to its kind, and everything that creeps on the earth according to its kind. And God saw that it was good. Then God said, "Let Us make man in Our image, according to Our likeness; let them have dominion over the fish of the sea, over the birds of the air, and over the cattle, over all the earth and over every creeping thing that creeps on the earth." So God created man in His own image; in the image of God He created him; male and female He created them. Then God blessed them, and said to them, "Be fruitful and multiply; fill the earth and subdue it; have dominion over the fish of the sea, over the birds of the air, and over every living thing that moves on the earth.

Born to be Wild

FIRST OFF, PARENTS, PLEASE NOTE THAT the cradle God created for His firstborn was rough country—a thorny, critter-laden and butt-kicking badland. God wanted His boy brought up in undomesticated surroundings. The feral fashioned something in God's first boy, Adam, that Xbox, the mall and cell phones just couldn't provide to the charge under His tutelage.

Yeah, God's earthy 2IC was directly connected to the Spirit of the Wild. Adam lived in primitive partnership with untamed beasts, birds, big lizards and monster sharks. This is the way it was. And God said, "It is good!" Imagine that: good being equated to having no anti-bacterial gel, no bike helmets, no Trans Fatty acids, no poodles, no motorized scooters, no concrete and no Dancing with the Stars. I know this doesn't sound like "paradise" for post-modern pantywaists that are immoral, lazy, stupid and fat, but it was God's—and His primitive son's—idea of "Yippee Land."

So what do we learn from this preliminary little Bible nugget, children? The lesson is clear: if you want your boy to step away from the pusillanimous pack, then you might want to get Junior outdoors, beyond the pavement, and let the created order carve its mark into your son.

I don't have boys, but I made certain when my two alpha teen-aged females were growing up that they had a regular dose of the irregular wild. Our lives consisted of large quantities of surfing in shark infested waters, biking in the backwoods, workouts on the beach, hunting in the sweltering swamps of the everglades for wild boar, fishing the brimming waters of South Florida and treks into the African bush. Why did my wife and I make the financial commitment and time-laden efforts to get away from the Miami metropolis? Well, call us weak; but we needed it for our souls, our sanity and our spirits in this increasingly plastic place. The spiritual and ethical moorings that nature affords us cannot be found in the tame and lame waste-lands of civilization.

So, take the time, No, make the time, parents of the peculiar Y chromosomes – to venture out with your boy away from the city, away from the tidy and predict-able, and watch what happens to your son as he separates from the prissy and is forced to interface with the primal. It is magical.

In the next few pages I'm going to look at God's view of what your son was meant to be and do as opposed to what this stu-pid society is attempting to make him be and do. Hang with me parents and you'll see how God hardwired your son to be a wild man, a ruler, a steward, a dragon slayer, a wise man and a son who reflects the grandeur of God and how it is your job to fuel this flame which, by design, burns in your boy's heart.

Doug Giles Tip # 2

Look to the Bible for examples of real men.

PART II
RAISING BOYS WITH MASCULINE VALUES

MASCULINE VALUES ARE VANISH-ing from within our nation faster than a Chimichanga dipped in motor oil would zip through your digestive tract. A myopic Cyclops can see that. Look, if you're a girl or a girlie man, well then . . . this is your day, Girlfriend. So, get on with your bad self. Girl power, girl power, girl, girl, girl, girl power!

I'm sorry, I got caught up in all the emotion and kinda lost it there for a sec. Now, where was I? Oh yeah. The neckerchief wearing "progressives" are ruining their new manicures working hard to have our nation Nancified. Make no mistake about it: misandry (man hatred) is now the dominating motif of the American milieu.

If you're the parent of a son and you want your kid to be a boy in the traditional, non-gender- blurred sense of the word, then you're going to be busier than a one armed wallpaper hanger finding and keeping good masculine examples for your young son. As I stated in the last chapter, good luck finding holy testosterone in Hollywood, in government schools and in the ridiculously feminized evangelical world.

The day has come when you, as a parent, are going to have to be defiant for your son's masculine rights and upbringing. The man haters have an ideological agenda and some prescription med's ready to rid your boy of all his distinct behavioral traits, and it's your job, mom and dad, to make certain these jackasses don't lay their gloves on him. Pink Floyd's "Hey, teacher, leave these kids alone" line from "Another Brick in The Wall" takes on a whole new meaning in this new millennium as far as sons are concerned.

One great source for rebellious inspiration comes from the Bible. The scripture is a great font for prissy, culture-defying fodder. In the scripture you see the men being men, and the demons being scared. You don't have to wade very far through the holy text before God starts laying down His blueprint for the boys. You find God's plan in book one, chapter one.

Gen.1.26-28:

Then God said, "Let Us make man in Our image, according to Our likeness; let them have dominion over the fish of the sea, over the birds of the air, and over the cattle, over all the earth and over every creeping thing that creeps on the earth." So God created man in His own image; in the image of God He created him; male and female He created them. Then God blessed them, and said to them, "Be fruitful and multiply; fill the earth and subdue it; have dominion over the fish of the sea, over the birds of the air, and over every living thing that moves on the earth.

What does God want His kid with balls to be? Well, here are six of the characteristics: a kid who is comfortable in the wild, who's ready to rule, is a savvy steward, is a dragon slayer, pursues wisdom and reflects the image of God. Having covered the necessity of the wild in your kids' upbringing in the previous chapter, let's check out God's desire to make him a conqueror.

Born to Rule/Take Dominion

God's initial earth boy was born to dominate creation and to exercise authority over the planet. God designed His first terrestrial son to be a leader, to take charge, to exert influence. God didn't construct Adam to be a passive clod, some indolent handout addict who abnegates his responsibility to other people or institutes; but rather, Adam was to be a bold and imaginative chief. This is the very thing the man-haters hate in men and are trying desperately to curb in your kid, namely, this can-do spirit.

Parent, you should encourage your bambino to lead, compete and conquer. Whether it is subduing his backyard, his dirty bedroom or an opposing team, or mastering a musical instrument, a textbook or a chore – your son should learn to govern, be the champion and strive for excellence in accomplishment in all that he does.

Look, according to the scripture, your son is a natural born leader who will naturally want to control. It is only, and I mean only, when boys are cowed by abusive authority, Ritalined out of their brains or indoctrinated to believe this God-given behavior is bad that they turn into the followers, the veritable sheeples of stupid cultural morays, folding to high pressure peers and ideological bullshit. With the leader funk removed from their trunk, now the boys become tofu for the man haters. Now they become malleable little spongy play things and are no longer steel-willed competitive leaders. Yes, they become nice, placid cooperators and doormats to fools and foes. God never intended a boy, your boy, to be this.

Therefore, parent, your job is twofold: 1) Unleash the leadership beast within your boy and 2) Superintend it to make sure it doesn't get weird; rather ensure it is used for the purpose of justice, truth, provision and protection. Take God's lead and show your son how to exercise dominion rather than how to get in touch with his feminine side. Maw and Paw, stand against the swill of society that seeks to erase this grand masculine trait from your little treasure and teach that kid how to be a constructive conqueror.

Doug Giles Tip # 3

Parents need attitude
and inspiration to blow off
the feminist funk.

PART III
RAISING BOYS IMPERVIOUS TO FEMINIST PRESSURE

FYI TO MOTHERS AND FATHERS OF boys: it is open season on your son in our gyno-centric culture, and the feminists are pushing hard for a no-closed season and no-bag limit. If you're a parent of a boy and would like him to retain his masculine distinctiveness, you might as well go ahead and buy the family HazMat suits because you're dealing with a feminist philosophy that is hazardous to your boy's masculine health.

The feminists and the men who have yielded up their private parts to the lesbians, I mean feminists, have an organized system of male hatred that they just can't wait to slap your son with. They're out in stretch pant force in Hollywood, our school systems and in limp churches with one goal in mind: to turn your son into a dandy they can direct.

The primary message of our increasingly jacked-up, feminized nation is that there is nothing about men that is good, or even acceptable. Guys get tolerated nowadays only to the extent that they yield to the cultural castration. To the feminist, the only good man is either a dead one or a neutered one.

Get it right mom and dad, your son is the Nuevo piñata of postmodernism, and according to the Ms.'s, their sex is to blame for all societal ills. For the dasypygal misandrist matriarchs, men are but a necessary evil whom they'd like to silence and dehumanize. And to make it fun for the fem's, they've made men the brunt of all of their jokes. Speaking of jokes, why are you so touchy, feminists? What has happened to your tough skin? Jeez, Louise. I can't even tell a joke about a woman any longer without NOW coming over to my house and unscrewing all my light bulbs.

Case in point: I was at the Miami

Improv the other night watching two comedians, one man and one woe-man. Both comedians told jokes that took jabs at the opposite sex. The female, a semi-funny, chunky has-been said, "my mom always said men are like linoleum floors. Lay 'em right, and you can walk all over them for thirty years." All the women roared with laughter, and my buddies and me grinningly agreed. Then the male counterpart took the stage and said, "women are like cow dung: the older they get, the easier they are to pick up." The men of course hit the floor laughing, but the women, the women, let out a deep growl of disapproval. It was as if the co-median said he'd like to eat a deep-fried kitten for dinner or something. Seems like these girls can dish it, but they can't take it. Oh well, back to my original screed.

To counter the organized hatred of men and masculinity that your son is facing it's important that you, the parent, completely blow off all of the smack our PC-addled culture is trying to sell you. You'll need two things to do this: attitude and inspiration. You can get the attitude by buying my book, *The Bulldog*

Attitude, and you can get inspiration and directives for your boy's masculine upbringing from the Holy Bible.

As the title of this chapter denotes, this is part three in a series in which we're looking at Genesis 1-3 regarding raising boys instead of some liberal University's Gender Studies class.

In Genesis 1.26-3.16 we see God's intention for his first boy. He was:

1. Born to be Wild

2. Born to Lead

3. Born to Cultivate

4. Born to Slay Dragons

5. Born to be Wise and

6. Born to Reflect the Majesty of God.

Having covered one and two in my previous chapters, here's my dig at point three: Born to Cultivate.

The Garden of Eden that God allotted Adam was not some dorm room that he was licensed to trash, but a place he was "to tend and keep" (Gen.2.16). Adam was to cultivate that which he had subdued. With his leadership came the responsibility and accountability to God to take that which was under his care and make it better. Can you say better? I knew you could.

This means, mom and dad, it's cool for you to have expectations of your kid about his role in your family and in this game of life: it is to enhance that which is good and to not whiz on everything people have worked for. Let little Johnny know that whatever gets tossed to him is to be brought it into greater order, usefulness and beauty. Make sure he gets the message that he's to do it. You heard me, him. Johnny. Not the government, not mommy, not his nanny, not his church, or his lawyer – Johnny is to get his act together. Johnny is to make the place shine. And Johnny is to feel really bad if he does not make things better and people prosper.

Therefore, parent of he that liveth in the God-blessed testosterone fog, train your son that he is not free to use, abuse, abandon, desert, ignore, overlook, disregard, forget, avoid, mistreat or neglect that which gets placed under his care; and if, if he does, he is to have his backside whupped. What am I saying? Your boy needs to slowly begin to feel the weight of masculine responsibility on his shoulders and learn how to get his skinny legs strong enough so that he doesn't drop it. BTW parents – it won't crush him. He's tougher than you're being led to believe.

Discipline your boy to fend for himself and others as if there were no government, no church, no school, no courts, no therapy, no drugs and no cops to lean on to make things all better. Yeah, raise him to feel as if it is his duty to be the provider, to educate his children, to defend his family and nation, to judge disputes, to offer worship, to give spiritual advice and comfort, and to do all of this without acting like a chick.

The wild thing that'll happen is you'll see little Johnny turn into big John who brings to the table more than waxed eyebrows and manicured hands and who's always looking to the ladies to lead him. Instead, you'll have raised a son who brings to the table emotional strength, physical toughness, firm correction, world wisdom, constructive criticism and ethical principles, and one who does it while having a heck-of-a-lot-of fun. This cultivating spirit will, by fiat, make him a leader wherever he happens to go and you know, you know, the long-toothed feminists will really, really, really hate that.

<u>Doug Giles Tip # 4</u>

Raise your son to be a
dragon slayer.

PART IV
RAISING BOYS WITH THE MASCULINITY OF CHRIST

FEMINISTS WOULD LOVE NOTHING more than to take your son and eradicate his masculine uniqueness. They hate men, and therefore, they will hate your son. That is, of course, assuming that you, the parent, intend to raise your son to be a man instead of a rouged and lipsticked, male American Idol hopeful. Get it right, parental unit: in the coming days you will be facing female chauvinist pigs who have sick designs for your dear son in culture, in the classroom and in a lot of churches.

These whacked women actually believe that masculinity, the male composition, and a guy's hormones cause boys to become wicked oppressors, sexually abusive and brutal beasts; and they have the inflated stats, the re-written history books and the hysterical spin to prove it.

These wizards (or I guess that would be witches if I'm going to use the black magic reference correctly) think they must help you with your little devil. They're trying to get you to raise your son as a girl, totally blowing off the fact that he isn't a fair lassie, insisting he should become like one because, women, and women alone, have the cure for our planet's ills.

The female chauvinist pigs do not mind you having a niño as long as he is purposefully dwarfed into growing up to be a malleable male complete with man boobs and dependant upon mummy. However, their chauvinism will show its ugly mullet head once you wisely concede to let nature take its decisive course and turn that male kid into a conqueror.

For the parents who have determined they are going to rage against the chauvinistic vomit of the shemales, you're going to need some help in the form of books to give you wisdom to buck the sinister system of the cynical sisters. Get my book, The *Bulldog Attitude*, to help you perfect the masculine spirit of your son. Get Harvey Mansfield's book, *Manliness,* to get a clear understanding of what you, as a parent, are up against in raising a son in a society that seeks to raze him. Get Leon Podles' book, *The Church Impotent*, to grasp why the Church has turned a paler shade of pink. And finally, grab a Bible to get God's 411 on how to righteously rear your son.

The "irrelevant" Bible's relevance for manly child rearing is particularly pertinent during this day of emasculation. The fem's not only find men insufferable, but they're also repulsed by the Bible because it puts the "go" in the male gonads. For instance, in the first three chapters of the book of Genesis, we see how the Designer designed His boy to be competent in the wild: a confident leader, who is to be a profitable park ranger over creation and a slayer of dragons. Having examined the first three musts for parents to instill in their sons in the previous pages, here's volley number four: Born to Slay Dragons.

In Genesis chapter three, when our first parents got tossed out of the sweet haven of Eden's crib, God said He was going to redeem this hamartialogical mess by raising up a Son who is to crush the serpent. Where God's first man, Adam, blew it by not being the dragon slayer, His second man, the Last Adam, took care of business and turned the malevolent slithering one into a grease stain.

If you as a parent take your cue from Christ in raising your son, then your boy will grow up to be a mini-me slayer of serpents. He will not be a pacifist in the face of evil. He will not roll over and wet himself when confronted by evil crap. He will not play the wimp when faced with difficult situations.

Look, I know it's hard for some of us to square Christ with slaying dragons – given all the androgynous, soft-focused paintings of Jesus that we've had jammed into our psyches for the last few centuries. However, if, if, you take the scripture straight (as I do my whiskey), the man of peace is painted as an eschatological warrior who has great joy in giving the devil hell. No matter how hard the softies try to make Christ out to be the benign, bearded lady raconteur, or a 19th century

liberal, or a 21st century feminist, the ex-
egetical fact remains: if you take the holy
text in its entirety, He does not fit into
the effete mold.

Therefore, mom and dad, have your
boy get used to confronting nonsense –
first and foremost in himself. Gear him
up to be a fighter and defender of that
which is just and good. Let him play,
as one author said, with toy weapons
instead of Barbies (if you can find any).
He's not going to turn into a terrorist. It's
not going to warp his wheel. Your son has
to learn that he is growing up in difficult
times that demand he be able to deal with
"snakes." Yes, your boy needs to learn not
only to be nice, but also to be strong,
sacrificial and courageous. You know, the
very God-given and nature-expected stuff
that the female chauvinist pigs are seek-
ing to sift from him.

Doug Giles Tip # 5

Teach your son to
be articulate, well-read
and wise.

PART V
PARENTS OBSESSED WITH TEXTING + IGNORED KIDS = HELL TO PAY

CAN YOU IMAGINE THE UPROAR THAT would rightfully ensue if Hollywood produced a movie that painted black people as idiots that white people had to help or they just couldn't make it through life? Or what if Tinsel Town got their best and brightest together to spit out a flick that framed Muslims as violent, religiously illegitimate zealots with glazed over eyes that must be quickly kicked to the global curb? Whaddya think the Islamic reaction would be? Huh?

Or, what if TV writers and producers took a turn and started cranking out sitcoms and commercials that pitched women as dense, manipulative, unfeeling and vicious whores? I'm talkin' about one show after the other where women are depicted as insipid bottom feeders who follow only the dictates of their lower cortex monkey brains and whose only hope for escape from their innate ignobleness is through totally yielding to the Zen of men. How do you think the ladies would respond to such an egregious assault upon their fair sex? I can tell you how: with claws out.

The above mentioned bigoted and unthinkable cinematic scenarios are exactly what men who wish to be men – and not women – get assaulted with day after day in the entertainment industry, on the university campus and in a lot of churches. The clear message that comes from popular culture is that masculinity sucks, and femininity is fabulous, even for men. Men who would be men are getting pounded in pop culture and everyone is expected to be cool with it.

Look, I know guys aren't perfect, that we're a scratchin', fartin', beer, sex and gadget driven gender. I can laugh at our stupidity and knuckle dragging tendencies, but it has officially gone over the top from poking fun at male foibles to a nasty, systematic, organized bigotry cranked out by feminists towards men that would not be tolerated if it were even mildly volleyed at women, at a particular race or a specific religion. And you know I'm spot on.

This leaves two options for parents of boys who want them to become men: 1) capitulate to the current cultural castration in raising their male kid or 2) rebel against the emasculating metrosexual machine. I suggest rebellion – unless you're cool with your son acting like JLo.

In order to rebel you need a vision of what is preferred and a blueprint regarding how to proceed. That's where the most hated book by the female chauvinist pigs comes in, i.e., the Bible. You don't have to unpack the scripture too much until you start getting the message that God created men to be wild, to lead, to make life better for everyone, to slay serpents, to be wise and to reflect His majesty (Gen.1-3). Having tackled the first four topics in my last chapters, here's my run at numero cinco.

Born to be Wise

ONE WAY TO FOMENT THE FEMALE CHAU-vinist pigs is to make sure, mom and dad, that your son is incredibly smart. You must make certain that he not only has a well-fed wild streak, a willingness and ability to lead in life, that whatever he gets his hands on prospers, and that he will tackle evil wherever and whenever it raises its ugly head, but that he is also the most well read boy on the block.

Parent, if your son stays dumb (and I'm not referring to children with learning disabilities) then he boosts the malicious stereotype that the fem's are shoving up our society's tailpipe, and he unwittingly sets the stage for a worse mañana, at least as far as masculinity goes. Mom and dad (and especially dad), don't give the female chauvinist pigs any ground by pitting one form of masculinity (leading) against another form (reading).

Parents, teach your rough and ready boy that:

1. Serious studying is not just for Poindexters and geeks.

2. Studying, learning and holding intellectual discussion are all part of being masculine.

3. The intellectual target you're aiming for him to strike doesn't look like Tommy Boy or Homer Simpson; but rather more like King David, William Wallace and Sir Winston Churchill.

4. It takes guts and nuts to tackle the various sciences and no matter what his idiot friends think, serious study is not for pussies. As a matter of fact, it is just the opposite. Reading, meditating, gaining understanding and knowledge and staying abreast of what has happened and what is happening on this world's stage is so hard that the effeminate, the little Sally's, the prancing, petite male poodles won't do it; they actually avoid it like Rosie O'Donnell does Jenny Craig.

5. God intends for him to be sharp and to not be a bastardization of his great gender. Then, Daddy-O, go to work to get your kid a killer library. Spend the cash!

6. The rowdy realm of ideas and debate can be just as fun as any sport. It fact, one of my greatest joys is when I get to go toe-to-toe on the radio, TV or over dinner with a flaming liberal or raging atheist. Yeah, it is right up there with hunting Africa's green hills, nearly.

Finally, parent, can you imagine the angst when Hollywood and the multitudinous, hijacked-by-feminists universities can no longer play the stooge card when it comes to men because the sons you have raised have engaged their brains and have not opted for anti-intellectualism? Can you picture, mom and dad, how the faces of the female chauvinist pigs will contort and how their stomachs will gurgle with acid as the stereotype they've worked so long and hard to prop up no longer works because you, the parent, have raised your son to be intellectually astute?

I have a dream!

Born to Reflect the Majesty of God.

PARENTS, ONE GREAT WAY TO HAVE Johnny not turn into a dandy is to take serious stock of the male role models he's around. Your son is going to imitate someone, so make certain it isn't some tool. This is not rocket science. But it is a science. It's simple: if you don't want your son to be emasculated or macho-stupid, be careful who you allow him to walk with on his schlep. Monkey see, monkey do.

BTW, can some of you girls stop imitating guys? Please? Like . . . now? The other day I saw this Hispanic chick cruising on a Harley. Her gut was hanging over her way-too-low-cut jeans, she had a cigarette dangling from the corner her mouth, and she was sporting more tattoos than a Maasai warrior. I had to do a double take because I thought it was my gardener with a wig and some Frederick's inserts. Yikes!

Also, girls, if you want to celebrate your "freedom" from misogynist's constructs by smoking a cigar, don't smoke a .62 ring gauge maduro Churchill. Stay somewhere south of .36. I know you're not supposed to trust men; but trust me—you'll look better.

Now, back to role models for your son. Even I have role models in case I drift to the effete dark side. There are eight in particular who help me keep my testosterone in focus and my boys intact.

1. Larry the Cable Guy. He keeps me tethered to my beloved redneck roots that are under constant attack down here in the oh so sassy South Florida. Git-R-Done, Larry.

2. Dennis Miller. Miller keeps the wise guy alive and well in me, which is a must if you want to mess with the FCPs and have the attitude necessary to navigate the Sargasso morass the feminuts spew forth.

3. Ted Nugent. Ditto. The Nuge also brings to the table an enviable love for hunting, guns and all that is wild and free. His music, books, concerts and our conversations keep my primitive man in fine shape.

4. Os Guinness. He takes the dumb out of Christendom.

5. R.C. Sproul. He is an apt destroyer of atheistic nonsense and a brilliant communicator of the essentials of Christianity.

6. My dad. He loved one woman, raised four kids and put them through college, and was a sharp, solid and smart man.

7. Several dead guys for several reasons. To name a few: Winston Churchill, Nicolai Fechin and Thomas Paine. And last but certainly not least . . .

8. God. I know following His flawless lead is most of the time an exercise in futility, but the Unseen One is a great example of masculine uniqueness. He's wild and He's wise . . . a warrior, a king, a prankster, a healer and a father. We are made in His image and should reflect his glory.

Now, my personal role models might not be the ones you'd choose; but the point for you as a parent is to be one for your son—and get some others who will help you forge your son into the force he's been called to become. Mom and Dad, by simply taking control (taking control, taking control) of who your boy hangs out with, what you let him watch, read and listen to, you can help him find his masculine groove and pursue it with vigor while blowing off the effeminate funk of the FCPs.

Addendum: Parents Obsessed with Texting + Ignored Kids = Hell to Pay

This past week I saw a sad sight. No, it wasn't Eric Holder trying to convince us that he's now a terror exposing hero instead of the perpetrator of a deadly Mexican gunrunning op that had its sights set on ultimately getting our Second Amendment rights revoked— though that was pretty sad, as that dog wag had all the subtleties of a Chaz Bono rumba.

What eclipsed that miserable moment (sorta) and caused me grief this week was watching a young mom at Starbucks ignoring her beautiful, little one-year-old girl while said moron giggled and texted for 30 plus minutes.

Yep, with her head buried in the phone, nose two inches off the cancer screen, mommy dearest didn't have a clue what her kid was doing as she crawled around on a high traffic, grime-laden cement floor between the feet of strangers who held 16- ounce cups of 180 degree liquid above the kid's tender flesh as they high stepped over her.

Hey, parents, here's a freebie from Dr. Doug: Why not put the cell phone and gadgets down for awhile when your babies are around and pay attention to them, all right, jackass? There'll be plenty of time later in life to ignore them—like in college, when they pierce their nipples and become whiny liberal drips, but now, when they are very young, is not the time.

FYI to Y-O-U, mom ... dad: You've got one shot at raising that baby, and if you want to make certain your spawn doesn't:

1. Recite hate poems about you at Barnes & Noble's open mic night regarding how they'd like to stab you in your sleep for ignoring them for the last sixteen years.

2. Show up high as a kite at a NYC Flea Party Rally, bitching and moaning about hard work and shouting up Che Guevara's *weltanschauung* as they roast a fatty ...

... then you might wanna give junior some TLC while he's a T-O-T. You dig?

As I watched this neglect go down at Starbucks, I kept thinking that this daft dame could have cooed and cuddled with her little bambina and had 1,800 seconds of parental bliss that lovely morning.

The Starbucks I visited was on beautiful Miami Beach. Mom could have pointed out to baby the seagulls, the palm trees, the gorgeous skies, the warm sun, the six-foot three-inch trannie with a five o'clock shadow, the rats rummaging through the trash eating discarded ham and cheese paninis, and the ubiquitous metrosexuals with over-tweaked eyebrows who use seven words to order their special cup of Joe. It could've been both a bonding and educational familial exchange in one warm whack. But no. The bird *had* to text.

Here's a challenge for the parental units: If you think I'm full of crap in regard to the ramifications of blowing your kids off as you obsess with texts and/or social media then let's do an experiment: For the next 13 years abandon the developmental stages of that genetic concoction of yours, and we'll see how they turn out as you snub them for Twitter. Are you ready? Okay. On your mark. Get set. Go, Slingblade!

Oh and by the way, conservatives and evangelicals ... you, too, can be dilatory dillweeds as this sin knows no party or religious affiliation. I know stacks of family values blowhards out there yapping about the importance of family who haven't talked to their own family in the last few weeks. Hey, dork, save your house first ... then talk to us about ours. I know way too many ministers who strode forth to save the world and lost their kids in the process. Didn't the apostle Paul say something to the effect that if you can't govern your own house then you need to shut the hell up?

And finally, if my exhortation to selfless and sacrificial love for your kids versus your gadgets has failed to convince you to change your behavior toward your toddlers, perhaps a selfish plea will. Soon, parents, in the not too distant future, you will return to the dependent state from whence you came, and I'm a guessin' that the child you ignored while he or she was in diapers will more than likely return the favor when you are sporting Depends.

About the Author

Doug Giles is the man behind *ClashDaily.com*. In addition to driving *ClashDaily.com*, Giles is a popular columnist on *Townhall.com* and the author of the book *Raising Righteous & Rowdy Girls*.

Doug's articles have also appeared on several other print and online news sources, including *The Washington Times*, *The Daily Caller*, *Fox Nation*, *USA Today*, *The Wall Street Journal*, *The Washington Examiner*, *The Blaze*, *American Hunter Magazine* and *ABC News*.

He's been a frequent guest on the Fox News Channel and Fox Business Channel as well as many nationally syndicated radio shows across the nation — which, he believes, officially makes him a super hero.

Giles and his wife Margaret have two daughters: Hannah, who devastated ACORN with her 2009 nation-shaking undercover videos, and Regis who is an NRA columnist, huntress and Second Amendment activist.

Doug's interests include guns, big game hunting, big game fishing, fine art, cigars, helping wounded warriors, and being a big pain in the butt to people who dislike God and the USA

Other books by Doug Giles

Ruling in Babylon: Seven Habits of Highly Effective Twentysomethings (2003)

Political Twerps, Cultural Jerks, Church Quirks (2004)

The Bulldog Attitude: Get It or Get Left Behind (2006)

10 Habits of Decidedly Defective People: The Successful Loser's Guide to Life (2007)

A Time to Clash: Papers from a Provocative Pastor (2008)

If You're Going Through Hell Keep on Going (2009)

Raising Righteous and Rowdy Girls (2011)

All Doug's books can be purchased at www.clash-daily.com

Speaking Engagements.

Doug Giles speaks to college, business, community, church, advocacy and men's groups throughout the United States and internationally. His expertise includes issues of Christianity and culture, masculinity vs. metrosexuality, big game hunting and fishing, raising righteous kids in a rank culture, the Second Amendment, personal empowerment, politics, and social change. For availability, email <u>clash@clashdaily.com</u>.

66265747R00034

Made in the USA
Lexington, KY
08 August 2017